Delaware River

Delaware River

George L. Spector

Frank Amato
PORTLAND

River Journal

Volume 6, Number 4

George L. Spector was introduced to fishing by way of his maternal grandfather who took him fishing while George was growing up in Japan. The mountainous regions of Japan are home to many native species of char and salmon. Fly-fishing for native char species, such as the "yamame," is very popular and enjoys a rich and storied history. George moved to the United States to attend college at age 18. During college, George fished extensively throughout New York State, namely the tributaries of Lake Ontario, which receive annual runs of salmon and steelhead. Today he makes his home in New York, where he is not far from the legendary rivers of the Catskill Mountains. He makes trips to his favorite river, the Delaware, as often as he can. In 1997, George received the status of Master Fly Casting Instructor from the Federation of Fly Fishers.

Acknowledgments

Thanks to Dr. Floyd Franke and John McCullough of the Beaverkill Angler for their help and guidance; Joe McFadden for his wisdom and unselfish help in sharing his knowledge of the Delaware. Special thanks to my father William Spector for rising early in the mornings to take me to my favorite bass pond in my youth.

Series Editor: Frank Amato
Kim Koch

Photography: George L. Spector (unless otherwise noted)
Fly plates photographed by: Jim Schollmeyer
Design: Jerry Hutchinson

Softbound ISBN: 1-57188-264-2; Hardbound ISBN: 1-57188-265-0
(Hardbound edition limited to 350-500 copies)

Frank Amato Publications, Inc.
P.O. Box 82112, Portland, Oregon 97282
(503) 653-8108
Printed in Singapore
1 3 5 7 9 10 8 6 4 2

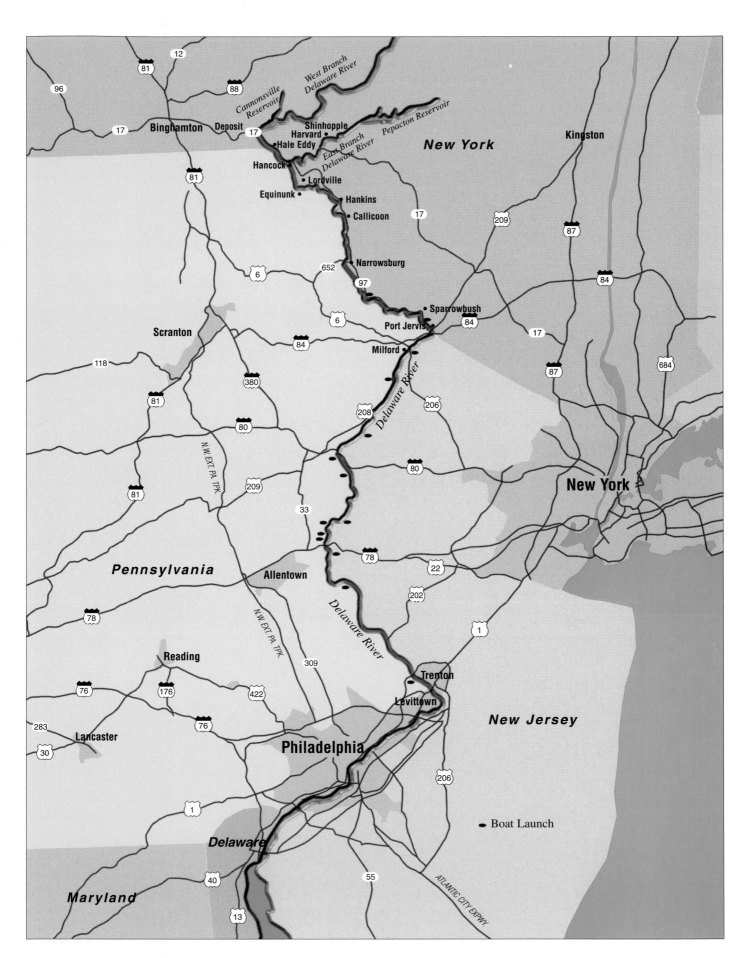

Delaware River System

In *Trout*, Ernest Schwiebert describes the Delaware fishery as, "the finest fishery in the eastern states, the big water on the Delaware between Hancock and Long Eddy. It is a river of swift half mile riffles and mile long pools, and only twenty-five years ago it held a population of smallmouths and walleyed pike....after the completion of the Pepaction Reservoir above Shinhopple, on the East Branch of the Delaware, the river can run cold and strong from the dam tail waters to the sprawling riffles above Port Jervis. "...that evening we fished a sweeping waist-deep riffle that surged past our waders in the twilight, and when a heavy hatch of big Isonychia drakes came off in the shallows, the big rainbows started rolling and slashing on top." Schwiebert also says, "Since the Cannonsville Dam was filled on the West Branch of the Delaware above Deposit, the main river below Hancock and Fishes Eddy receives another source of cold dam tailings. Its population of big rainbows is remarkable, and there are fly hatches of incredible diversity and numbers.....we fished one of these mile-long flats one evening in late summer, hooking a half-dozen fat rainbows that accelerated downstream on blistering runs that spooled deep into the backing. It is not easy fishing. It calls for willingness to wade deep; and the double haul is almost mandatory."

History Of Settlements

Human settlements along the Delaware date to the last 10,000 years. Ancient bands of people foraged on fish and animals which inhabited in and around the river basin. Scientists have also found Indian tribal remains along the Delaware River dating back to around 2000 BC. According to the "Upper Delaware Journal" these Indian tribes called Lenni Lenape inhabited the region for centuries where they flourished on abundant food supplies and ideal habitat.

European settlements along the Delaware River date back to about the early l600s when a group of Finnish and Swedish people made portions of the valley their home. Up until that time, the river valley was used only as a trading route. The first major settlement was established around the town of Cochecton (then called Cushetunk, meaning redstone or stone hill in the Indian language). Early settlers found well-marked Indian trails which enabled the Europeans to interact with neighboring establishments and eventually travel to the upper Delaware region.

It is thought that the majority of the present-day population of people in the upper Delaware region originally came from the southern Connecticut area. Early European settlers used Indian trails to migrate from Connecticut in search of land. In the early 1700s, European settlers ventured westward into Indian Territory in search of land for farming. Connecticut's land ownership system was comprised of freeholders. In other words, "men owned their land and were free to do with it as they pleased. This was not the case in all of the colonies. The Dutch who settled in the Mamakating Valley in New York, for instance, did not own the lands on which they settled. Rather they held them under a feudal system which required that they pay rent to the landowner or landlord. These people, then, had little incentive to expand their landholdings, since they didn't own title to the land. Freeholders, on the other hand, had every reason to increase their holdings, since the size of a man's homestead was an indication of his wealth and standing in the community."

By the middle of the eighteenth century, the colony in Connecticut became overcrowded which caused a shortage in good farming land. The farming way of life necessitated a large

The quaint community of Downsville was settled in the late 1700s. It is situated only a mile or so from the Pepacton Reservoir.

Historic covered bridge spans the upper East Branch in the town of Downsville.

The sign at the Pepacton Reservoir clearly marks the intended use of the water supply.

family to do the work in the fields. This overpopulation made land ownership especially difficult for young families, who were left with little choice but to seek newer grounds. "All of the lands between the Connecticut River and the Housatonic River, right up to the boundary of New York, was already being heavily farmed, and the western part of the colony was also feeling the pressure of an increasing population." Moreover, in those days, farmers had no idea of the necessity of alternating their crops so as not to strip the land of nutrients and cause the erosion of topsoil. The grounds simply wore out due to over-farming, causing a reduction in their harvest.

The UDJ states that "the citizens of Connecticut believed that the boundary of their colony continued westward beyond the horizon, they felt they were perfectly within their rights to migrate and settle on lands of their choice any place west of the Delaware River within the north-south breadth of their home colony." At the time, neighboring states as well as the indige-nous Indian tribes claimed that the region of Cushetunk belonged to them.

When the original explorers of the European colony returned home to Connecticut, they gave reports of finding a beautiful land and valley where they could make new establish-ments. This new land found along the Delaware River would increase their wealth and feed their families for generations. This allowed the establishment of the Delaware Company and the formation of the Upper Delaware River settlement.

History Of The Fishery

Prior to the construction of the Pepacton Reservoir in 1954, the East Branch of the Delaware River was a warmwater fishery. Summertime water temperatures reached into the low 80s. A 1936 NYSCD study showed that species that dominated the river were walleye and pickerel. According to the Region 4 NYS DEC (New York State Department of Environmental Conservation) report, "A History of the Fishery Resources in the Upper Delaware Tailwaters," some trout, consisting mostly of browns, inhabited areas of riffles and influxes of cold springs.

The construction of the dam created a fine tailwater fishery until a severe drought in the 1960s minimized water releases and adversely affected the fishery. Trout populations diminished as daytime water temperatures increased to intolerable levels.

The West Branch was essentially a warmwater fishery as well until the construction of Cannonsville Reservoir in 1963. However according to Kay Sanford of the NYS DEC, the West Branch was actually warmer than the East Branch, making it less suitable for trout and smallmouth bass, which were the primary species.

Releases from Cannonsville Reservoir were often unpre-dictable (0-2500 cfs) as a result of trying to meet the down-stream minimum flow requirements. These "erratic" flows damaged both coldwater and warmwater fisheries. Therefore, according to Kay Sanford, fishing opportunities were at a minimum during the earlier years of the dam construction.

The NYS Legislature enacted a law in 1976 regulating reservoir releases to accommodate environmental require-ments that gave the DEC the power to govern over 31 reser-voirs, including those controlled by New York City. This legis-lation improved reservoir releases and the fishery of the Delaware. One study biological survey conducted in 1935 showed that both rainbow and brown trout were established in colder sections (around tributaries and springs) of the main river. In its hay day, the main stem was considered the best smallmouth bass river in New York State.

Section below the Downsville Dam is off limits to fishing.

The East Branch

The construction of the Pepacton Dam at Downsville in 1961 created a fine tailwater fishery, the East Branch of the Delaware River. The East Branch, however, can actually be divided into three sections, each with its own distinct characteristics. The stretch above the reservoir is a quaint little freestone harboring 9- to 12-inch browns, which are mostly stockies. Easy wading and abundant fish populations make this stretch an ideal choice, especially for novices. There are some large browns that are caught in the fall during their spawning migration up from the reservoir. Fishing various feeder streams, such as the Batavia Kill, Tremper Kill and Platte Kill, may produce an occasional lunker.

The upper stretch below the dam, which runs about sixteen miles, resembles a spring creek. The river consists mostly of long and glassy pools with weeded bottoms which harbor abundant populations of insects and crustaceans. Brook trout dominate the upper stretches and brown trout increase in population further downstream. Large brown trout, some up to 26 inches, are taken from the East Branch, especially

Section of the East Branch around the town of Harvard. This area is known for large brown trout.

Stretch of the East Branch around the town of East Branch, New York. An angler tries his luck below the riffles.

*Clear water conditions on the upper stretches of the East Branch call for stealth and
ultra-delicate presentations. Large brown trout inhabit these waters but are difficult to catch.*

Diner and grill located in Fish's Eddy on the East Branch of the Delaware River.

Branch," on Route 17 will put you onto Route 30; then, travel upriver toward the Pepacton Reservoir. There are some riverside campgrounds located on the East Branch and by staying there, access to the river is naturally granted. This is an excellent way of fishing some private water on the river. Although much of the water is posted, access is fairly easy; look for these access sites especially around the several bridges located on the river.

The section of river from the town of East Branch, where the Beaverkill River meets the Delaware, to the town of Hancock where the East Branch meets the main Delaware measures about seventeen miles. This stretch resembles a freestone and although it appears promising, it is actually a poor trout fishery. The benefits of the cold water releases from the Pepacton do not reach as far down and the infusion of warm water from the Beaverkill does not help matters. By the middle of June, most trout leave the lower stretches or seek thermal refuges to escape the heat of the summer months. Therefore the lower stretches of the East Branch are best fished in the spring and fall when water temperatures are more ideal and hospitable to trout.

Access points on this lower section can be found along River Road that parallels the East Branch and also at exits found on Rt. 17. The Shad Pool located on Rt. 17 just past the town of East Branch has been a favorite of many trout and shad anglers for years. The area around the bridge at Fish's Eddy as well as at

by those who are adept at stealth approaches and matching the hatches. Anglers wishing to challenge large trout should try fishing the section between Shinhople Bridge and the bridge at Harvard.

Access to this section can be found along Route 30, which parallels the river. Getting off at the exit, "East

Two anglers discuss the day's strategies for fooling the difficult trout of the East Branch.

Don't overlook obscure pockets above pools and along grassy banks and around small islands.

Hancock (Rt. 97) offers good rainbow trout action as these species are prevalent, especially in the early season. McCarter's Hole below the bridge where Rt. 17 crosses over the river is an excellent spot to try for rainbows. Try crossing the river and fish the entire pool, especially at the riffles and pocket water.

The West Branch of the Delaware is perhaps the premier tailwater fishery in the Northeast. Stable cold water flowing from the Cannonsville Dam has established a rich ecosystem with abundant and diversified insect life creating a trout fisherman's heaven.

Another good spot is the pool below the town of East Branch, above Bolton's Eddy. The bend produces good fish. This deep pool is excellent holding water and best fished from the east side; however, when the water is high, it is nearly impossible to cross the river.

There is also excellent holding water at Pea's Eddy where there is a large island and numerous brooks which enter into the river. Don't overlook obscure pockets above pools and along grassy banks.

The West Branch

The West Branch of the Delaware is perhaps the premier tailwater fishery in the Northeast. The construction of the Cannonsville Dam in 1967 created a coldwater trout fishery for 33 miles of the West Branch. It is a river of abundant and diversified insect life, which is both a curse and a blessing for the prospecting hatch-matcher. The maintenance of cold-water flows creates an ideal habitat for fish and insect life, its smorgasbord of hatches necessitating an exact imitation and precise presentation. This challenge created the birth of new patterns, such as the Comparaduns made by two "Delawarites," Al Caucci and Bob Nastassi in the 1970s.

The section of the West Branch above the Cannonsville Reservoir runs a whopping 45 miles. This section of river mostly passes through farmland from which nutrients run off into the river

11

A stretch of public water located along Route 30. Although much of the river is posted, access is fairly easy, especially around bridges.

A nice brown trout taken at the factory pool located in the upper West Branch. West Branch is known for large brown trout up to 33 inches!

and in turn into the reservoir causing an algae bloom in the summer months. Foot-long, stocked brown trout predominate this section, and offer easy and relaxed fishing. This upper section is accessed from Rt. 10, which parallels the river from Walton and Delhi to Stamford. Look for state access sites that are clearly marked; ample parking should also be found around bridges as well.

Access to the east side below the Cannonsville Reservoir can be gained by using Route 17 and there are also some county roads on the west side of the river. Access is fairly easy and there are a few PA and NY sites along Penn-York Road. Most float trips are usually made between the no-kill stretches of Deposit down to Balls Eddy state access site. The float can be

Early June is a perfect time for taking big fish. Nighttime emergences of big Acroneuria *stoneflies and* Pteronarcys *salmonflies make for tasty morsels for big fish.*

Jim Serio getting ready to drop his drift boat at the Stylesville access site. Float trips can be made with pontoon or drift boats as well as with canoes. You can rent boats at some local fly shops listed in the back of this text.

Walking along a farmer's corn field in Deposit can access a very productive pool below the factory pool.

browns. By late May, water levels are usually low, making the river easily navigable and more hospitable. There is no admittance at the section from the Cannonsville Dam to Stilesville; however, from Stilesville to the Rt. 17 bridge, there is good access and good water. There are several pools which hold fish and this section is definitely worth a try since it does not get as crowded as the no-kill stretch just below.

The no-kill section is located from the Rt. 17 Bridge down river for two miles. According to the NY DEC personnel, this stretch probably holds the most number of fish (about 1000 per mile) and the largest in the West Branch during most of the season. A good place to try is a large pool located below the Rt. 17 Bridge. This pool which is located in Deposit (get off at the "Deposit Exit" on Hwy. Rt. 17) is easily accessible by parking along the road which parallels the West Branch. There is also angler's parking on the lower section of this stretch and by walking through the corn field or along the river bank, another very productive pool can be accessed. There is an excellent pool before a bend in the river (which should be fished on the other side of the corn field) and a large pool past the bend.

A "rules and regulations" sign posted along the special catch-and-release-only site of the West Branch. Many fly anglers prefer to fish these special waters because of the numbers of fish as well as the larger sizes of the trout.

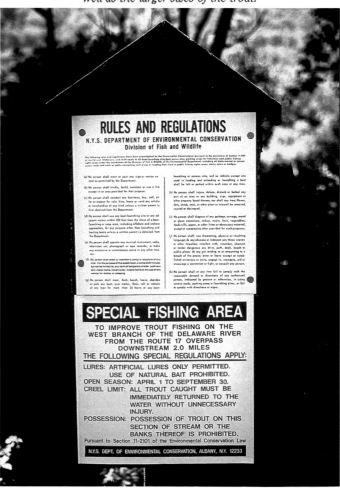

made by pontoon and drift boat as well as by canoe. This trip will take a person all day to make but can be cut in half, allowing more fishing time, by taking out at the Hale Eddy Bridge. Because there is currently no boat ramp at the bridge, a pontoon or canoe is ideal for this shortened expedition.

The West Branch is known for very large fish and a 33-inch whopper of a brown was taken in the no-kill stretch in 1998. Some large fish are taken during springtime when water spills over the top of the Cannonsville Dam bringing alewives into the river. Anglers should fish very large white streamers (i.e., Zonkers in size 2) on sink-tip lines (200 grain is preferred) along the banks and around grassy knolls, ideally from boats during high water. The fall is also an excellent time to catch some very large trout. When spawning browns make their annual migration up the West Branch from the main river, it presents an opportunity to angle for big fish. Large Muddler Minnows, in sizes 4 to 6, should be fished deep with sink-tip lines in pockets and around shoals below small islands. Work your way up from the lower portions of the river as spawners make their migration upstream. Keep in mind that after September 30, you can fish the West Branch only up to the NY-PA border waters.

The time of the Brown and Green Drake emergence and spinner fall sometime in early June also presents a perfect opportunity for taking big fish. An added bonus during this time is the nighttime emergence of *Acroneuria* stoneflies (best imitated by yellow Stimulator patterns in size 8) and big *Pteronarcys* salmonflies (in size 4). Anglers braving the night are sometimes rewarded with 20- to 24-inch rainbows and

The main Delaware meanders around hills, flows through four states, and finally empties into Delaware Bay.

The main Delaware is characterized by a series of long and deep pools. It is a river with mile-long pools that resemble small lakes.

The pool at Hale Eddy Bridge is very productive, though at times very crowded. Some anglers prefer the deeper water below the bridge since good fish tend to hold along the bank on the west side of the river. I have had good luck at the head of the pool as well as below. You can also walk upstream from Hale Eddy after crossing the bridge to get to a very good pool located below a bend.

Downstream from Hale Eddy begins the "border waters," where on the west side, the river is bordered by the state of Pennsylvania. There is good access (angler's parking is marked by Pennsylvania) along the road which parallels the river. The "Gamelands," as it is referred to, contains miles of good fishing water.

In Hancock, easy access is found at the bridge on Rt. 191. This pool gets fished heavily but is also known to hold big fish. Work your way down from the fast water on top (from the east side) to the deeper section below. Good fish tend to rise just out of reach on the far side of the deep section and a boat is needed to effectively present the fly. Moreover, the current slows in the tail out of this pool just to make things more difficult.

The Main Branch

The Main Branch of the Delaware River is formed by the confluence of two tailwaters, the West and the East Branches of the Delaware. From the Junction pool in Hancock, New York, the Delaware meanders around hills where towering conifers abound, flowing through four states and finally emptying into Delaware Bay. However, it is the first twenty or so miles which harbor decent wild-trout populations, consisting mostly of browns and rainbows. Summertime releases from the Cannonsville Reservoir keep water temperatures fairly cool but only for a few miles downstream of Hancock.

Rainbow trout were first introduced into the Delaware by an Erie railroad brakeman, Dan Cahill, in the 1880s. The initial plan for Dan Cahill was to transport and stock trout into the West Branch of the Delaware; however, the train broke down around the town of Callicoon and rather than have the trout die, he dumped them in a nearby creek. Not until the construction of the two bottom-releasing dams did the rainbow trout proliferate and expand its range into the headwaters of the Delaware.

The main Delaware is characterized by a series of long and deep pools. During heavy water releases, the "Big D," as it referred to by Delaware River regulars, resembles a giant spring creek. With its grassy banks and huge boulders that occasionally spot the river bottom, the main stem is big water with huge, mile-long pools that resemble small lakes. Trout are all wild in the Big D and its rainbows are legendary

Access site located in the town of Callicoon, New York. This is a popular site for drift boat anglers wanting to fish the lightly fished lower sections of the main stem. Many canoeists use this site in the summer months.

in their blistering runs, often peeling off yards of backing. Large fish often sip small insects off the top in "chum lines" created by eddies and structures. Precise hatch matching is a must and frequent refusals by seasoned fish are a common occurrence. Delaware's water is relatively calm and flat and

You can easily get a shuttle service from one of the local fly shops. The Shehawken access site in Pennsylvania is a popular launch site on the West Branch.

The Buckingham access site in Pennsylvania is a popular take-out point for many anglers wanting to fish the West Branch and the main stem.

so can be intimidating to the novice angler. Learning how to fish a large river with flat water can be difficult and so hiring a guide for a float trip on a McKenzie style drift boat is highly recommended.

The Delaware watershed between Callicoon and Hancock is an expansive area. There are some access points, especially around bridges. However, much of the property is privately owned. There is access at Callicoon, at Kellums Bridge, at the Lordville Bridge and in Hancock (at the water treatment plant). There is also a boat launch site at Long Eddy as well as at Buckingham, which is in Pennsylvania.

Most spots are accessible even during medium-flow conditions. However during high-water conditions, such as in the spring and during heavy water releases, the Delaware is best fished from a boat. You can either use a drift boat, canoe, or a pontoon boat to get you from spot to spot. Or by using an anchor, you could easily position yourself to where the fish are holding.

Although most of the riverfront property may be privately owned, you can fish many miles of the Delaware River by launching a canoe or boat. This is because the bottom of the Delaware to the high water mark is owned by the state. When using a boat, plan your float trip ahead of time by using a map.

You can easily get a shuttle service from one of the local fly shops for a reasonable fee. Ideal floats are usually made from Balls Eddy access to either Sheehawken access on the West Branch or from either access down to the Pennsylvania Buckingham access on the main river. Keep in mind that the run between Balls Eddy on the West Branch and Buckingham is an all-day affair whereas the trip from Sheehawken down to the main stem can be made in a half day (usually evening trips). Naturally, the amount of time you spend fishing can lengthen the trip. Also keep in mind that all boats must have valid New York or Pennsylvania registration and floatation devices equal to the number of passengers.

Successfully fishing the Delaware requires an angler to sharpen his casting and presentation skills. Success on the

Delaware watershed, however, depends largely on two factors: Fly patterns that are better suited for flat water and presentation.

Important Mayfly Hatches

There are many species of mayflies that inhabit the Delaware watershed. Due to their abundance, some are more important than others for the fly-fisherman. The following is a list of important mayflies in the Delaware River.

Quill Gordon

Epeorus pleuralis, or Quill Gordon, is an early season hatch, usually occurring in mid-April. Nymphs inhabit the oxygen-rich fast waters and bolt to the surface during their emergence. They are fast swimmers and anglers can best imitate their emergence by allowing a wet-fly imitation to swing downstream and rise up at the end of the presentation (i.e., Leisenring swing). An effective way to fish this "miserable weather fly" is to cast a duck-quill winged wet fly upstream and allow it to sink. As the fly swims downstream, twitch it to entice the fish into striking. At the end of the swing, twitch the fly again as it rises up toward the surface. This famous hatch can last to mid-May during some seasons. I have found that hatching can occur when the water temperature reaches and is sustained at around 50 degrees. Unfortunately, pollution and siltation has restricted the range of these mayflies in the Delaware.

I have experienced good hatches of *pleuralis* species on the lower stretches of the Delaware, especially around Callicoon. However, the unpredictability of the weather in the early season makes this hatch a very difficult one to fish. Quill Gordons have been known to hatch on cold and windy spring days. Try to stick to days with warm afternoon temperatures for more predictable hatching activity.

Paraleptophlebia adoptiva: The Blue Quill (#16-#18) is a very prolific hatch which usually occurs around the end of April to the beginning of May. These small mayflies can stir up tremendous activity in the early season; I have experienced excellent fishing on the West Branch of the Delaware where hundreds of *adoptiva* mayflies were bringing trout into a feeding frenzy. The hatch on that day lasted from 11:00 a.m. to around 1:30 p.m.

At times they appear on the water at the same time as sub-varia species, therefore great care must be taken to inspect which species the fish may be keyed in on. *Subvaria*, which is larger than the *adoptiva*, may draw the angler's eye but it may actually be the latter that the trout are feeding on.

The Hendrickson hatch is perhaps the most anticipated hatch of the early season. Here anglers try their luck at a deep pool located in the special regulations section of the West Branch.

Ephemerella subvaria: According to Caucci and Nastassi, there are as many as six subspecies of Hendricksons in the Delaware River. They range in sizes from 9mm to about 12mm. The hatching activity of *subvaria* species usually occurs around the end of April to early May and can last to the middle or the end of the month.

The Hendrickson hatch is one of the most anticipated early-season hatches, many anglers eagerly await their arrival all winter. The hatch is considered very reliable, usually occurring around 2 p.m. lasting until 4 or even 6 p.m. (Hatching normally commences when the temperatures reach 50-55 degrees). Many guides on the Delaware advise their clients to fish Hendrickson nymphs in the morning and early afternoon; they automatically switch to dries around 2 p.m. whether or not the duns are actually present on the water. Such is the reliability of this prolific and much anticipated early-season hatch.

It is interesting to note that Doug Swisher and Carl Richards make the following observation in their book, *Selective Trout*. They say, "coloration of the Hendrickson dun can vary tremendously from stream to stream-in fact, even from different areas on the same stream. The suggested pattern for the subimago has a body constructed of yellow, tan and live fur, which is normally effective, but should actually be matched to the naturals being imitated. For the wings, the proper shade of gray should be selected from the mallard shoulder area."

Ephemerella rotunda: The red quill or dark Hendrickson normally hatches between the middle of May to early June. They run in sizes from 12 to 14. The *rotunda* closely resemble the *dorothea* species, however, the former are easily distinguishable by their larger sizes. *Rotunda* species normally hatch between noon and 6 p.m.

Ephemerella dorothea: Sulphurs hatch on the Delaware sometime between the end of May to the middle of June. Duns hatch on warm (and hot) afternoons and evenings around 7 p.m. Many anglers have a special affinity for Sulphur hatches since these small mayflies hatch under ideal conditions when the river is low and wadable and the weather warm. Authors Caucci and Nastassi make this observation in *Comparahatch*: "Fly-fishers are kept constantly off balance by the ability of these insects to turn hatching activity on and off like a faucet. Blizzard-like hatching between 7 and 8 P.M. one evening might be followed the next day by a sporadic three-hour emergence in the afternoon. During the earlier hatches, emergence might take place in later afternoons or early evening, but will usually occur after 7 p.m. Later, as the weather gets warmer, hatches will most likely occur just before dusk except during cool, unseasonable

An angler tries his luck at the pool in Kellum's Bridge. This pool, as well as pools located downstream around Callicoon, are a favorite of many who fish the Sulphur hatch in early June.

Vitreus nymphs inhabit the well-oxygenated fast water at the heads of pools. Look for them hatching in riffles and turbulent water. Here George Menda hooks into a bullet train on a stretch of fast water on the East Branch.

weather when premature hatching might occur during the afternoon.....there are, no doubt, many factors which contribute to the confusing emergence behavior of these mayflies..."

It is important not to confuse the *dorothea* duns with those of the *invaria* and *rotunda* species. These groups of

Gray Foxes, which are related to March Browns, hatch some time in mid-May to June in good numbers on the Delaware. Hatching activity can be heavy on the West Branch.

mayflies all look similar but the trout may be keyed into a specific hatch.

Because *dorothea* nymphs become very active just before and during hatch time, be sure to carry an ample supply of nymph patterns. Anglers most often fish *dorothea* nymphs in early June due to the species' abundance in the river system and switch over to dries when hatching activity commences. Splashy rises should be fished with effective emerger patterns dressed with snow-shoed rabbit fur or CDC.

I like fishing the lower sections of the river around Callicoon for the Sulphur hatch. When the water temperature reaches around 65 degrees the Sulphur hatch intensifies and brings up big rainbows in the evenings. Hatching activity peaks until the hot, early-summer sun warms the water to upwards of 72 degrees when trout activities subside.

Spinners fall at dusk and well into dark. Heavy fish tend to feed on *dorothea* spinners but can be very selective due to the abundance of other species during this time. Spinner patterns tied with white CDC wings are a favorite since they float well and can be easily seen on the surface by anglers.

Ephemerella cornuta: These Blue-Winged Olives, which run about a size 16, hatch sometime in early to the middle of June. They are an important species on the Delaware since

Unfortunately, the Green Drake emergence coincides with Memorial Day weekend in the Catskills, which usually signifies the start of the "aluminum hatch," the emergence of canoeists.

their prolific numbers bring up many trout. *Cornuta* nymphs generally inhabit the slower portions of the river but they can also be found in riffles. However, look for them to be hatching in slower pools and back eddies in the early mornings.

Epeorus vitreus: The heaviest hatches of *vitreus*, or Sulphurs, occur in June. Like their cousin, the *pleuralis*, *vitreus* nymphs inhabit the well-oxygenated fast water at the heads of pools. Therefore, look for them hatching in riffles and turbulent water. The *vitreus* duns closely resemble the *dorothea* duns; however, the former is a size or two larger and a shade darker. *Dorothea* also hatch in quieter parts of the river, or in flats and long, glassy pools.

Stenonema vicarium: March Brown hatches can be very sporadic and may not stir up much activity from the trout in the Delaware. Instead, a greater importance can be placed in the pre-emergent nymphal activities and spinner fall in the evenings. However, during good hatches, these mayflies can bring up good fish due to their large sizes. Look for them hatching, especially on cloudy days, in the afternoon from around late May to early June. With their large upright wings, the *vicarium* resemble small sailboats.

Stenonema fuscum: Gray Foxes, which are smaller cousins of the March Browns, hatch mid-May to June in good numbers on the Delaware. I have encountered excellent hatches throughout the Delaware system, especially on the West Branch. Since duns are light colored, they are very easy to spot on the water. This and their larger sizes make the *fuscum* hatch a pleasant one to fish.

Stenonema ithaca: Light Cahills hatch sometime in late June (peak period) and sporadically throughout the summer. During the hot summer days, look for these light-colored mayflies to be hatching in the mornings and late evenings. *Ithaca* hatches can be very sporadic and may not create much interest from the fish. Light Cahills become more important in the summer due to lack of activity from other mayfly species. Fish feeding on *ithaca* may be less selective due to hatching sparseness. Look for heaviest activity at dusk.

Ephemera guttulata: Without a doubt, the Green Drake is the most widely anticipated hatch of many anglers. It is certainly the most famous in the East where anglers eagerly await their arrival sometime in late May to early June. No hatch is more storied, stirring up interest from angler and trout alike, which rise to these tasty morsels with reckless abandon.

Unfortunately, the Green Drake emergence and spinner fall coincides with Memorial Day weekend in the Catskills, which usually signifies the start of the "aluminum hatch," the emergence of boaters on their canoes.

It is difficult to time the tremendous but short-lived Green Drake hatch on the Delaware. However, no other hatch brings up the biggest trout from the depths of the Delaware.

The main stem of the Delaware lacks large boulders and structures so fish the riffles and pockets for Isonychia *action. Splashy rises mean the rainbows aren't too far away.*

It is somewhat difficult to time the short-lived *guttulata* hatch, especially since they may hatch in the evenings. Contacts with local fly shops are helpful but flexibility in being able to hit the river with short notice is the best strategy in this case. I have encountered with some regularity the spinner fall of both the Green and Brown Drakes but not the actual hatching of these unpredictable species. All in all, the lucky angler who visits the Delaware and encounters the hatches (and/or spinner fall) of these magnificent species, is in for a thrill of his or her life. I can think of no hatch that can bring up the biggest trout from the depths of the Delaware River. Just ask Jim Serio who guides on the Delaware over 100 days out of the year. He hooked and landed two 24-inch browns one evening in 1999; he later told me that his friend, Richard Franklin (whose beautiful photographs of the Delaware have been published in major fishing magazines) forgot to bring his camera on that particular day! Coffin flies, or spinners of *guttulata*, return to the river a few days after their emergence. Swarms of adults laying their eggs on the river stirs excitement from the fish and fishermen. Be sure to purchase some coffin flies at local fly shops before venturing out to the river. Some fly patterns call for the use of porcupine needles for their abdomen (extended body). Unfortunately, frenzied feeding behavior by the trout is often short-lived.

Ephemera simulans: Caucci and Nastassi claim, "...we found very good populations on large rivers such as the East and West Branches of the Delaware River, as well as the main Delaware just below the town of Hancock, New York. The Delaware system has produced blizzard-like hatches, but of very short duration (3-5 days). Unfortunately for the weekend angler, it is very possible to miss this hatch completely if hatching takes place during the week."

The brown drake's spinner fall can occur around the same time as the *guttulata's*. Anglers must exercise caution so as not to mistake the two species that are similar in size. The fish may be keyed in on one species and completely ignore the other. Capturing a specimen becomes very important in such a case.

Ephemerella attenuata: These size 16 Blue-Winged Olive species hatch in early June and can last to the middle of July. These species are a major hatch in the Delaware. According to Al Caucci, like the early *Epeorus attenuata* hatch under water where many fall victim to the trout. Therefore, nymphs and emergers are effective patterns to fish this hatch. Look for these species to be hatching in the morning in the slower parts of the river.

Tricorythodes: Because the lower sections of the main river are too warm during August when the Tricos hatch, fishing is

Various Baetis *species are very important for the Delaware angler.* Baetis *hatch throughout the spring, especially in slower portions of the river. Look for them hatching in tailouts, such as this slow pool located below the Fish's Eddy bridge.*

restricted to the portions above Lordville and the West Branch. These tiny black mayflies, which hatch in the early morning, present a challenge for the angler but when fished correctly, it can be very rewarding and satisfying.

Baetis: The various *Baetis* species, which comprise this diverse group, are of paramount importance for the Delaware angler. *Baetis* hatch throughout the spring under various conditions. *Vagans* hatch in mid-April and can last into May. During this time, dry fly activity is restricted to warmer days but do not overlook nymphing as an alternative. Hare's Ear Nymphs tied with tungsten bead heads are deadly. Early-season high water due to run-off can make things difficult, so stick to pockets along shorelines and eddies with detritus. If trout are rising but refuse your offering, switch to emerger patterns for results. Trout that break the surface may actually be taking sub-surface emergers or submerged pre-emerging duns that are just under the surface film.

Pseudocloeon: These ultra-tiny Blue-Winged Olive species run from sizes 24 through 28 in the Delaware River. They can be observed hatching in the slower sections, where selective trout pick off these tiny morsels on the surface at their leisure. Their small sizes obscure their importance for the Delaware angler.

Pseudocloeon hatch in great numbers in many nutrient-rich tail waters and the Delaware is no exception. Although these species hatch in good numbers throughout the summer months, they are especially prevalent from the end of September through the end of October. Trout feeding on *pseudocloeon* hatches can be very selective because of the abundance of these insects. A slight variation in size or color can make the difference between a hook-up or refusal by the trout. Therefore, it is important to carry good imitations in various sizes and colors. Some veteran anglers prefer fishing this hatch over others because of the satisfaction they feel hooking a large trout on a small fly. Al Caucci, master of the Delaware, recommends fishing the hatch with low-silhouette patterns. He observes that many *pseudos* are either stillborn or have great difficulty keeping upright. Therefore, a lower-profile fly pattern better imitates this hatch.

Isonychia bicolor: I have a particular affinity for fishing *Isonychia* nymph imitations in the riffles. Large trout await the *Isonychia* nymphs to float by their lair behind boulders and submerged logs. These carnivorous creatures are lightning-fast swimmers; they hatch above the water, on stream structures, throughout the summer months. Their hatching activity peaks around June in the Catskills.

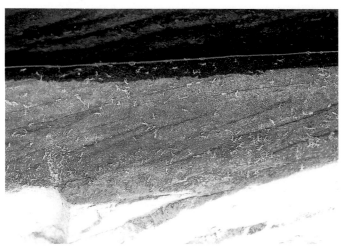

When nymphal shucks are observed on structures and banks of the river, try using bushy dry-fly patterns. You may be pleasantly surprised by some explosive action.

The Delaware lacks large boulders and structures which protrude above the water, therefore, pockets and riffles are ideal spots for fishing *Isonychia* flies. Be sure to fish undercut banks along the edges of the river as well as deeper water below any embankments. Wade softly and don't hesitate to become a stalker.

When nymphal shucks are observed on structures and banks of the river, try using a bushy dry-fly pattern on the fast water and be ready for the explosive strike from a rainbow. I like using Art Flick's Dun Variant with plenty of floatant for these situations.

Potamanthus distinctus: The emergence time of this species (July and early August) limits the location of fishing this particular hatch. This is because the lower portions of the main river are too warm for trout as are the sections of the lower East Branch. To fish this hatch successfully, one must stick to sections above Lordville on the main and the West Branch of the Delaware River. These large mayflies, which can run as big as a size 8, hatch in the evenings gen-

Mayflies aren't the only insects trout feed on in the Delaware River, dragonfly nymphs are also important food sources for Delaware trout.

erally after dark. This can be a very challenging hatch to fish since success means being able to coordinate in the dark.

Ephoron leukon: These large, white mayflies also hatch during the summer months in the dark. I have heard of excellent hatches in the Callicoon area but with no trout taking them being that the water was simply too warm. Lucky for the mayfly, by August when *leukon* species hatch in the lower portions of the river, most trout have moved upstream in search of cooler waters. That is not to say *leukon* does not inhabit the cooler waters upriver. In fact, in late August and September, *leukon* hatches provide an excellent opportunity to catch some big trout which lose their inhibitions at night.

Heptagenia hebe: These reddish-brown mayflies range in size from 6-8mm. They hatch between July and October and are particularly important in the early fall. Although *Heptagenia* hatches can be sporadic, fish seem to key in to their emergence. *Heptagenia* nymphs inhabit both fast and medium currents. Look for these flat-bodied nymphs to be migrating to slower sections of the pool before emerging.

Low-Profile Fly Patterns

Traditionally hackled Catskill patterns excel in riffled water. They are designed to float high and stay buoyant. Delaware's flat water, on the other hand, requires the use of flies which float lower on the surface film. "Low-profile" flies present a better silhouette and imitate more closely the emerger stage of the mayfly. There are many fly patterns which fall under the category of low-profile flies that are effective on the Delaware. In *Selective Trout*, Doug Swisher and Carl Richards claim that the most effective fly to emerge from their studies was the no-hackle fly. In the book, they remark that insect legs play a minor role in their general outline. "This fact prompted a close-up study of standard artificials, where we noticed that hackle was a ridiculous imitation of legs. It was not only too bushy but also obscured the outline of both body and wings. Instead of being the least significant feature, as it should have been, it was by far the most significant feature. The obvious solution was to cut down or eliminate the hackle altogether. This we did, and when combined with fur bodies, split tails, and various wings, the new no-hackle flies produced results far superior to those of flies we had ever tried."

Selective Trout popularized the no-hackle patterns and these flies in turn revolutionized the low-profile theories. Swisher and Richards' innovative ideas led the way for the creation of other low-profile patterns which are so effective in catching fish.

When tying the no-hackle patterns, the authors recommend splitting the tail fibers apart so that they serve as outrigger supports and properly position the fly on the water. On smaller flies, they recommend using turkey-body feathers, which make the task of making the wings much simpler.

Comparaduns were developed by Caucci and Nastassi on the Delaware River. In their book, *Hatches II*, Caucci and

Al Caucci and Bob Nastassi observed that the Delaware's relatively calm waters necessitated the use of a hackle-less pattern such as the Comparadun in order to imitate duns that are "riding the current peacefully."

Nastassi write, "...if the water is relatively calm and the duns are riding the current peacefully, a hackleless pattern such as a Comparadun, which features a distinct wing silhouette, would be the correct choice."

In *Hatches II*, Gary LaFontaine remarks that the Comparadun is really a "refinement" of the Haystack fly. However, unlike the delicate quill wings of the no-hackle, Comparaduns use more durable and practical materials for making the wings of the fly.

Comparaduns are effective in the early season for imitating large mayflies, such as Quill Gordons (size 12 and 14) in late April and Hendricksons (12-14) and *Paraleptophlebia* (16) in early May. Comparaduns can be used for large Sulphurs (12 and 14) in mid-May to early June and for Cahills (*Stenonema* and *Stenocron* 12 and 14) in late May through early August. In late May through early June, Gray Foxes (10 and 12) hatch in fairly good numbers. Comparaduns are easy to tie in larger sizes and can be fished in riffled water providing that you use good floatants or desiccants. Although sporadic in their emergence, *Isonychia* (size 10 and 12) is a favorite hatch of many during summer months. Look for them hatching in fast water in and around exposed rocks, in the late afternoon and evening.

Comparaduns can be tied to imitate smaller mayflies such as *cornutas* (size 14 and 16) and *cornutellas* (18) in late April and May as well as *Heptagenia* (16 and 18) in the fall. When tying smaller flies, use snow-shoed rabbit hair instead of coastal deer hair (elk hair) for the wing material. The former is much easier to use in sizes smaller than 18. Hi Vis can also be used since it is a material that is easy to tie flies down to size 26. Hi Vis works especially well since it can be seen easier on the water. Z-lon can be substituted for the tail as a nymphal shuck but remember that Z-lon sinks so use it sparingly.

Flies tied with water-resistant CDC, such as the RS2, work very well on the Delaware. The CDC wing floats high while allowing the body of the fly to lie flush with the surface of the water. CDC is especially useful for tying small flies such as for sulfurs (*dorothea* 16-20) in late May through early June and early *Baetis* species (16 and 18) in mid April through early May, when the water can he high and a buoyant pattern's needed. How much a fly floats can be adjusted by using one, two or even three CDC tips as the wing. It is possible to design CDC flies to be used on riffled water by carefully clipping the leftover fibers and mulching them with dubbing material for the body of the fly. The CDC mixed in with the body will make the fly float like cork.

George Menda lands a nice rainbow on a stretch of the East Branch using an Isonychia *pattern. George is a nymphing master who loves fishing the* Isonychia *nymph in fast water. He's rarely far from his Bogdan reel during the fishing season!*

Some Octobers bring sporadic hatches of caddis and can be a time of excellent rainbow action on the main stem.

Actually a very productive pattern tied with CDC is the Cul-de-Canard Comparadun. Adult mayflies have a very crystalline body and since CDC does not add bulk under the dubbing, it is easier to tie a thin body. This is very useful when tying small Comparaduns in sizes 22 through 26 (*Pseudocloeons* from May through October and Tricos, size 24 and 26 in July and August). Make sure to tie in enough dubbing up front to secure the wing upright.

Thorax flies are very effective low-profile patterns. The sparse hackle dressings balance the fly low on the surface film while giving it some stability on riffled water. But keep in mind that the first thing that comes into view in a trout's window is the wing silhouette of the fly. The hackle dressing does obscure the silhouette somewhat so, tie the wings longer than is called for.

On smaller flies (size 16-22), use turkey flats for the wing; on larger flies, such as for imitating the Green Drakes (8 and 10), Brown Drakes (8 and 10) and March browns (8-12) in late May through early June, use hen backs. Some hen backs are almost a perfect match to the Green Drake's wings but can create a pattern which is very air resistant to cast. Make sure to add a little more line speed and shorten up your leader to accommodate the extra bulk on the fly.

Daiichi 2X-long hooks are ideal for tying larger flies, such as for the Drakes, *Isonychia* (bicolor size 12 during summer months) and the *Potamanthus* white fly (size 10). The long shank aids in imitating the extended body of the Drakes. Long-shanked flies are better than the extended body since the former does not spin as much as the extended body patterns when casting. So, there is much less twist on the leader. Mustad 4X hooks also work well, however Daiichi 2X-long hooks build flies which float better.

Various caddis species are prevalent throughout the Delaware system. Most notable species include the early-season black caddis (size 18) in April and the Grannom caddis (14-16) which hatch in early May. Expect both species of light and dark Grannom caddis, also referred to as the shad fly, to be hatching on the warm afternoons. Swarms of this *Brachycentrus* species can stir up some tremendous dry-fly action on the river; however, when the top-water action is slow, don't hesitate to try a sub-surface pattern, such as bead heads or LaFontaine Pupas. Look for the green caddis to be hatching in the latter half of May and in June. These early summer *Rhyacophila* activities can sometimes extend up to and beyond sunset.

Some Octobers bring sporadic hatches of caddis in sizes 14 through 16. This can be a time of excellent rainbow action on the main stem. Anglers must "hunt" for fish and make accurate presentations in likely spots as fall brings low water and challenging conditions. Expect the fall caddis activity to occur during the latter part of the day and sometimes until dark. However, activity may dwindle as temperatures decline and the window of opportunity will decrease. Therefore, it is advisable to fish the warmest part of the day.

"Low-profile" caddis patterns are tied without hackle that is normally spun on the body, such as with a Henryville Special. For this type of pattern, topping the body with either elk hair or CDC material is preferred. These simple caddis patterns ride low on the surface and work well both in riffled and slow water. Wrap a bit of tinsel on the body and/or add sparkle yarn on the tail as an attractor.

Presentation

Presentation is even more important than using the right fly when fishing the Delaware. Since the river is large, long casts are frequently made to reach rising fish. Windy conditions are quite common, a five-weight fished on a nine-foot high modulus graphite rod is preferred. As a rule of thumb, try to get as close as possible to rising fish. The shorter the line, the less currents will have to be dealt with and therefore, less drag on the fly. If long casts must be made, move up and above the target and make a quartering downstream cast. However, just before the fly lands, bring the rod back and allow the fly to land a few feet above the target. Then instead of mending, bring the rod gradually forward in the direction of the current so the line will not drag the fly. Moreover, strip out line to float the fly downstream; this allows a lot of water to be covered below with minimal effort. Just cast quartering downstream and start stripping out line without creating too much slack line in case you need to set the hook.

When casting upstream, you must be careful not to line the fish. Try to use the curve cast and bend the line to the right or left so the line will not drift over the fish. Try to use at least a 12-foot leader even under windy conditions. Instead of trying to mend the line on the water, use the reach cast and bring the rod down in the other direction of the current so a mend is automatically created.

Presentation is even more important than using the right fly. On a large river such as the Delaware, long casts are frequently made to reach rising fish. Unfortunately, windy conditions are quite common.

At times, releases are insufficient and the river can become very low and difficult to fish. Water temperature is a key factor for the Delaware River fishery.

During hot summers, heavy releases are made creating a thermal refuge for miles downstream from the dam on the West Branch. Cold-water releases reignite hatching activity and create a "second season" on the Delaware. This section above the factory pool in Deposit is almost too cold during heavy water releases necessitating anglers to place their bets further downstream.

Summer Releases

The Pepacton Reservoir, completed in 1955, and the Cannonsville Reservoir, completed in 1967, were built by New York City to enhance the drinking water supply. The NYS DEC has agreements with New York City to ensure "conservation releases" to maintain ideal trout habitat in the summer months.

The Neversink Reservoir (operational in 1953) affects the releases made by the two reservoirs on the Delaware River. This is because a 1954 Supreme Court Decree contains "diversion allowances" and specific requirements for water releases. The Decree specifies that New York City can divert upwards of 800 million gallons a day from the two Delaware River Reservoirs to establish a minimum flow of 1,750 cfs to be measured at the Montague, New Jersey gauging station. To clarify things, if more water is released from the Neversink, less water is needed from the two Delaware reservoirs providing that the requirements are met. Flows are governed not only by water releases from the three reservoirs but also by rain and run-off. In 1954, the Supreme Court Decree established the River Master to supervise releases for minimum flow requirements.

As mentioned before, summertime releases keep water temperatures cool but only for a few miles downstream of Hancock. On or about June 15, mandatory water releases from Cannonsville Reservoir are made primarily to combat saltwater encroachment many miles downstream in the Philadelphia area.

During hot summers, heavy releases are made creating a thermal refuge for a few miles in the main river. My records show that on days with substantial water releases (600 to 900 cfs), the water temperature between Hancock and Equinunk can get down to the 50s. Naturally when the Rivermaster calls for less flows (160-180 cfs considered minimal and 350-600 cfs being medium flows), temperatures will increase and trout move upstream to seek cooler waters.

As mentioned before, water releases from the Pepacton Reservoir (its primary purpose is for New York City drinking water) are insignificant and create a thermal refuge only for a few miles downstream of Downsville Dam. Unfortunately during the summer months, warm water from the Beaverkill flows into the East Branch and then into the main stem. This warm water has an adverse effect on the main river fishery as it combats the coldwater releases from the Cannonsville Reservoir. Therefore, drought years bring better fishing in the main stem since warm water flowing in from the Beaverkill and East

Water releases from the Pepacton Reservoir are insufficient and create a thermal refuge only a few miles downstream of the dam. Moreover, warm water from the Beaverkill flows into the lower East Branch of the Delaware. This section of the East Branch around Fish's Eddy becomes too warm during the summer for trout habitation.

Anthony Scolpino lands a nice rainbow on the main stem of the Delaware. During low-water conditions, stick to riffles at heads of pools where any hatching activity may entice rainbows into striking your offering.

Branch is minimized. Moreover, drought conditions down river in the Philadelphia area causes saltwater encroachment in their water table so heavier water releases are generally called for by the River Master.

Radio-telemetric studies conducted by TU and NYS DEC have shown that trout migrate upstream into the West Branch to seek colder waters during the summer months. Radio transmitters were placed into the abdomen of the trout; researchers were able to receive a signal up to 3/4 of a mile and therefore monitor the movements of the trout under study throughout the year. Fifty brown and rainbow trout, both hatchery and wild, were being studied. The study showed that 5 out of 6 trout in the East Branch left the river by early summer. Three trout migrated between 2 to 12 miles to the West Branch. One brown and one rainbow traveled upstream 13 miles to seek cooler head waters. By fall, four out of five trout returned to the lower section of the river. On the big river, trout moved out of the main stem into the West Branch by early summer. Rainbows, however, returned back to the main river by fall. In fact, one rainbow had traveled an incredible total of 60 miles throughout the year. The study showed that when releases are light or when the river temperatures increase, it a good bet trout populations in the main river begin to thin out. This is certainly the case in lower portions of the main Delaware (Long Eddy to Callicoon) where water temperatures can reach in excess of 80 degrees during very low flows.

The NYS DEC does not consider the sections of the river below the town of Hankins to benefit from the coldwater releases from the reservoir. Do not count the lower portion of the river out in the fall when cooling water temperatures

repopulate these sections with rainbows. Lower water levels, however, may take the difficulty of flat-water angling to new heights. Stick to riffles at heads of pools where any hatching activity may entice rainbows into striking your offering.

In June, when water temperatures begin to increase, conservation releases are made to maintain ideal trout habitat; however, at times, releases are insufficient and the river can become very low and difficult to fish. Water temperature is a key factor for the Delaware River fishery. Pre-release conditions can badly stress fish, especially if the river is low and warm. A few degrees make a big difference in the activities of fish; rainbows may be actively feeding at 65 degrees (ideal conditions) water temperature whereas in over 73-degree conditions, they are very sluggish and their feeding habits may become suppressed. One year in early June, I fished an excellent Sulphur hatch in Callicoon. At 67 degrees, rainbows were full of vigor and by the end of nightfall, I managed to hook and release two 20-inch bruisers. I fished the next consecutive evenings; water temperatures increased daily until the fifth day, it reached 74 degrees. Needless to say during these low water and hot early summer conditions, the river temperature swelled quickly and put a damper on the activity of fish. It's best to call local fly shops to get the latest conditions. You can also call (914) 295-1006 to get up-to-date water release information and future projections.

Shad

The sun was setting over the hill of the Delaware River. The air was warm and dry. My friend Jeff Brainard and I

A 6 1/2-pound shad caught in the main stem of the Delaware River around Callicoon, New York. The Delaware is known as the king of shad rivers.

hurried down the steep bank to the river. The previous day's rain swelled the river, but not enough to adversely affect the fishing.

When we got down to the river, Jeff quickly pointed out fish activity on the surface of the far bank. We saw shad darting, circling and breaking the surface in the slow water. There were about a dozen that we could see in the general area and many more downstream. We could see a few swimming in the current in front of us.

Jeff and I decided to fish the fast water at the head of the pool. I got into position and made a cast. The fly swung just at the seam of the current when a fish suddenly intercepted it. The reel screamed as the shad stripped off 50 yards of line in one powerful run. The line arced across the river as the fish came to a sudden halt and sulked on the far side. I applied pressure on him but, at the same time, remained cautious so as not to break him off my light tippet.

A half-hour later (and a few hundred yards downstream) I was able to net the shad, which turned out to be a six-pounder. I carefully removed the fish from the net and foam spilled from its shiny flank.

While releasing my fish, I saw that Jeff was busy fighting a shad of his own. He was elated and one could easily see how these silvery creatures that swim like bullets could indeed bring sheer excitement to any fisherman.

The American shad (*Alosa sapidissima*) is indigenous to the Atlantic coast of North America. It ranges from the rivers of Labrador to as far south as the waters of Florida. In the late-1800s, shad were introduced to the Sacramento River in California and are presently found along the Pacific Coast from Mexico to Alaska and Russia.

The American shad can be easily differentiated from its cousin, the hickory shad (*Alosa mediocris*), whose lower jaw protrudes beyond the upper jaw and is generally smaller (1-3 pounds) than the American shad (2-8 pounds). The largest American shad taken by hook and line is just over 11 pounds.

According to the NJDNR, close to a million shad enter the Delaware system each year making it truly the king of shad rivers. In early March, shad begin to collect around Delaware Bay; they move into the Delaware River by late March to early April when the water temperature rises to about 40 degrees. The shad then travel about 330 miles upstream to the town of Hancock, New York where the main stem separates into the East and West Branches. At the junction of the two branches, the majority of the shad swim up the East Branch, some all the way to Pepacton Dam. Even before the reservoirs were built in the 60s, shad seldom ascended the West Branch. While in many rivers the survival rate of spawned shad could reach as high as 50%, because the migration up the Delaware is so long and strenuous, the mortality rate could be as high as 95%.

*Tackle for shad does not have to be sophisticated;
nine-foot rod fished with a six-weight line is ideal.*

*Joe McFadden owns a fly shop in Hankins, New York.
He likes to fish for shad in the area of Kellums Bridge.
Angler parking is located on the New York side.
Try fishing the riffles upriver from the bridge.*

My initiation to shad fishing came as an accident some twenty years ago. While fishing a *dorothea* spinner fall one late-June evening, I hooked what I thought was a monster rainbow trout. After a fierce 10-minute battle (which included spool-clearing runs and cartwheeling jumps), the fish finally came to my net and to my amazement, it was a 5-pound silvery shad. I was not only surprised at the accidental catch but what the fish actively took. From the little I knew at the time about shad, I thought shad did not feed once they entered a river system. Many years and countless shad later, I realized this earlier notion not to be true.

Of the guides I consulted for this book, Tony Ritter out of Narrowsburg, New York, specializes in the river between Narrowsburg and Hankins. He prefers fishing with sink-tip lines in deep holes where shad tend to hold. He feels consistent hook-ups with shad has much to do with water temperatures, clarity and flow of the water. He likes to fish in water less than 4 feet since the pods of fish in shallow-water conditions are less dispersed and easier to fish to.

His choice of tackle includes a very fast sink-tip line and a five-foot leader tapered down 0X. Clouser Minnows (size 4) in color combinations of red/white, chartreuse/white and chartreuse/black fished quartering downstream in tailouts of riffles and heads of eddies work best for him.

His proven strategy over the years has been to "find an area of the river in where the fish get cordoned off into a slot so they are less likely to scatter and position in a tail out or base of the rapids where shad will hold before they make their run up the gradient."

Joe McFadden, who owns a fly shop in Hankins, New York, along the banks of the Delaware River, has been fishing for shad longer than he cares to remember. He likes to fish for shad in the area of Kellums Bridge because the area is close to

his shop. Earlier in the year, he uses 6- and 7-weight rods with sink-tip lines. He says, "the flies we use are little smaller than what is used in the lower river; I like 'em in size 6 tied with Krystal Flash." He also claims many miss some spectacular shad action later in the season by not fishing for them with dry flies. When the water level is low in June, for example, shad will often key in to a hatch or spinner fall. During this time, shad are caught accidentally by trout fishermen using a dry fly. According to Joe, a pod of shad working the surface on a specific insect can be just as selective as a trout. He recommends matching the hatch and going a bit heavier in tippet size than what is called for when fishing for trout.

Casting heavily-weighted shad flies requires special casting form. You must open up your loops to accommodate the extra weight and slow down your stroke. Pat Schuler, owner and operator of the beautiful Starlight Lodge in Starlight, Pennsyvania cautions all of his clients not to cast "these flies as though they were dry flies (or) you'll soon find one somewhere in your body. Also, if the heavy flies hit your fly rod, the rod will

The access site at Callicoon where Callicoon Creek empties
into the main Delaware is a favorite of many shad fishermen.
Try fishing pockets and runs around the bridge as well as
the deeper section of the pool down river.

usually break." He recommends lobbing the fly, keeping it away from the body and rod. Pat specializes in the area of his home base in Hancock but maneuvers around where the pods of shad are thickest. Because the shad are always on the move, especially earlier in the season, Pat covers a lot of water to find them. He fishes the entire river between the town of East Branch, New York and Callicoon.

Shad flies generally have two things in common: flash materials and bright coloration. Many prefer to build flies (such as the Clouser Minnow) which use lead dumbbells or bead-chain eyes because it enables the fly to ride upside down. This in turn aids in a more solid hook-up in the upper jaw of the shad. However, as discussed earlier, the added weight in the fly creates a pattern that is very difficult to cast, especially on windy days. The casting stroke must be altered so that loops will be wider to accommodate the extra weight. Many who feel uncomfortable casting heavy flies because of the danger, prefer to use sink-tip lines to sink the flies. In this scenario, just about any streamer with brightly colored bucktail or Flashabou will be effective.

The tackle for shad need not be sophisticated. Your basic trout gear will do just fine. I prefer a 6- or 7-weight line fished on a 8 1/2- or 9-foot graphite rod. Reels with rim control or one with a good drag are ideal. Reels with a click and pawl drag will suffice. Because most shad strip out line, make sure your reel contains at least 100 or 150 yards of 20-pound backing just to be on the safe side. Many anglers prefer to use a sink-tip line in order to present the fly to the level where the fish are holding. However, a weight-forward floating line will work providing that you use enough weight of the leader to bring the fly down. Full-sinking lines are not preferred because it can take the ability away from the angler to control his fly. Eight- to nine-foot leaders should be used in conjunction with floating lines, whereas a four- or five-foot leader will suffice when using sink-tip lines. Leaders should taper down to 4X or 5X.

There are a few types of presentations that work well for shad. The down-and-across cast, as used when fishing for Atlantic salmon, seems to work the best, probably because it effectively covers a lot of water. When employing this technique, make sure to dangle the fly downstream for a few seconds at the end of the presentation. Many a shad have succumbed to this offering. A technique that has become a standard for shad fishing on the Delaware is the down-and-across cast coupled with a shooting head and running line. I mentioned before that the fly must be presented at the depth where the fish are holding. The weight of the shooting head keeps the fly at a certain depth, even while you retrieve your line. Moreover, the narrow diameter of the running line minimizes drag on the fly. This technique works especially well when your fishing a deep pool or when the river is high from spring run-off and the fish are deep.

On a large river such as the Delaware, I find it helpful to employ what Doug Swisher calls the "mend-shooting" streamer strategy. In this technique, he casts up and across and immediately repositions the line on the water by shooting and mending downstream. In other words at the same time you mend, shoot some line out for the fly to follow across the river. You can also strip in line fast or slow as the fly makes its swing downstream. However, hold the line loosely with your right finger as you strip, in case a shad strikes hard. Doug Swisher's streamer strategy is a useful tool because it covers a lot of water.

Most hook-ups occur without actually setting the rod. Strikes are usually aggressive and the fish tend to hook themselves. Many novice anglers make the mistake of horsing the fish and end up pulling the fly right out of the fish's mouth. Since shad have soft tissue around the mouth, it is best not to apply excessive pressure.

Other Species

Although most of the preceding pages have been devoted to the two main game fish, trout and shad-there should be some mention of other fish species which also inhabit the Delaware watershed. Smallmouth bass are prevalent throughout the main river, especially the warmer sections down river, from Callicoon to Port Jervis (about 40 miles). They average about a foot in length but some are caught in the 2- to 3-pound range. Walleyes inhabit the deeper pools of the Delaware. They average about a pound-and-a-half and can reach in excess of ten pounds. A guide who operates out of Hankins, Billy Frazier (Upper Delaware Outfitters (845) 887-4853) reports that fall is an ideal time to hook onto some lunker walleyes in the 6-pound range. It is interesting to note that a NYSCD study in 1936 shows walleyes were not present in the Delaware until they were stocked in the mid-20s. Therefore, there abundance is a relatively new development (1935). Although not a fly-rod quarry, muskies are stocked in the Delaware. I have never seen nor caught a musky but hear that they are sometimes taken from a section of river in Narrowsburg, which contains the deepest pool on the Delaware. Pennsylvania stocks tiger muskies in certain sections of the river and regular muskies in others.

Striped Bass

Recovery of the striped bass in the Delaware came in the late 1980s when sewage treatment and discharge into the Delaware was improved (converted into tertiary) which increased the dissolved oxygen content. Due to lack of data not much is known on the migration pattern and reproduction of the striped bass in the Delaware. What is known is that some very large fish are being caught throughout the river, sometimes fish as large as one lucky angler's 36-pound 44 1/2 inch monster caught in 1996.

Joe McFadden reports that he has seen stripers up to 36 inches at Kellum's Bridge pool. They make excellent game to pursue with fly tackle. However, the striped bass fishery in the Delaware is still in its infantile stage. This is because the migration of striped bass into the upper stretches of the Delaware is a relatively new phenomenon. According to Bob Angyl of the NYS DEC, a very large, 40-plus-inch striper was caught by the DEC in Sparrowbush in 1991. This catch showed that large, breeder-class stripers migrate far up the Delaware River. Angyl claims stripers traditionally ascended the Delaware as far as Milford, Pennsylvania. According to an article by Philip Chase in the publication, the Upper Delaware, striped bass were once very common throughout the Delaware River. In fact, their abundance in the 1870s posed a threat to the juvenile shad population. However, like the shad, pollution and industrialization in the lower river led to the decimation of striped bass in the Delaware.

Most striped bass on the Delaware are caught from late summer into early fall at night. Heavy tackle, up to a 9-weight, is advisable. Large flies, such as Zonkers in size 4 and minnow patterns up to 1/0, are recommended. Most stripers are in the 18- to 28-inch size but on occasion a large fish will keep things interesting.

Many feel the need for the 28-inch size limit to be decreased to eighteen inches in the Delaware. Neighboring fisheries, such as in Pennsylvania where the limit is 20 inches and in the Hudson River where the limit is 18 inches, have robust striper populations even with lower size limits. Joe McFadden feels that creating interest as well as awareness for the striped bass in the Delaware is essential if one aims to promote this fishery. "A reduction in the size limit is an ideal way to create interest for the stripers," remarks Joe. "When people are required to release 10-pound stripers because they are viewed as undersized does not help to create interest for this fishery." One Pennsylvania Fish Commissioner would like to see a more drastic drop, down to 15 inches.

According to UDC representative Philip Chase, a Dr. Desmond Kahn conducted a study in 1998 where he concluded that the striper population in the Delaware should be considered as "restored." According to Dr. Kahn, the striped bass in the Delaware have already spawned in the lower stretches and have migrated upriver by following the herring. He feels that since there are resident striped bass year-round in neighboring rivers, such as the Susquehanna, the bass in the upper Delaware are also there to stay. Other fisheries biologists feel as Dr. Kahn does regarding the status of striped bass in the Delaware.

It is important to note that there is some concern regarding what the burgeoning striper population may have on other species in the Delaware. A dramatic decline in the juvenile shad population may be attributable to the growing striper population. One study reports over a 90% decline in fish passage at a New Jersey counting station. Trout, which congregate near river mouths during summer, may be susceptible to striped bass predation.

For those wishing to fish for species which inhabit the lower stretches of the Delaware, there are several access points located in this section of the main stem. For example, there are four designated sites located on the New York side: In Sparrowbush, Narrowsburg, Skinner's Falls and Callicoon. The first two are boat launch sites, the latter are "hand" launch sites. On the Pennsylvania side, there are access points at Matamoras, Zane Grey, and Damascus.

Bald Eagles of the Delaware River

A hundred years ago, over 70 pairs of bald eagles nested in New York State however, by 1960, only a single nesting pair remained. Eagle sightings along the Delaware river were very rare. The reduction in the bald eagle population was largely caused by the use of harmful pesticides, such as DDT. Loss of habitat as well as unregulated hunting also led to their demise. The enactment of the Bald Eagle Act of 1940 along with the banning of DDT in 1972 have greatly aided in the restoration of the eagle population. According to the Eagle Institute (845/557-6162), the Delaware River serves as an important region for the population growth of eagles. Every winter, over a hundred eagles migrate to the upper Delaware River region. Along the Delaware River, the eagles find plenty of open water where they can find food. There is also an abundance of tall trees where they can find nesting sites. Most eagles return north but an increasing number have established permanent residence in this region.

The Eagle Institute recommends the following viewing sites for eagles: Mongaup Valley on the Rio and Mongaup Falls reservoirs. They are both in New York State off Route 42. Route 97 in New York at Minisink Ford, Barryville and Pond Eddy. Around Hancock, eagles can be seen at Lordville, New York, Equinunk, Pennsylvania and the Pennsylvania Buckingham boat access. The Eagle Institute recommends mid-December to mid-March as the prime viewing season. Mornings and late afternoons increase the chances of eagle sightings.

Conservation

The Delaware River was not always as beautiful as it is today. Overpopulation and urbanization, especially in the southern portions of the river around Philadelphia and Trenton, caused the river to become polluted in the 1950s and 60s. Industrialization from steel mills, chemical factories and oil refineries along with sewage runoff from sprawling cities added to the pollution. In the early 1950s, parts of the

The Delaware River was not always as beautiful as it is today. Human encroachment puts pressures on the environment and wildlife.

Delaware were literally sewer. The degradation in water quality caused a huge reduction in aquatic life and bio diversity; the huge population of shad which acceded the river each spring had all but disappeared.

During the late 1800s, the Delaware River annually produced over 13 million pounds of shad. These were the largest harvests of any river in the Atlantic. However by the early 20th century, signs of trouble were looming. Records show that by the 1920s, shad harvest was down to only around 200,000 pounds. Overfishing, pollution and damming took its toll on the shad population. Studies point to pollution around the Philadelphia and Wilmington, Delaware area as the cause for the reduction in shad population over time.

In 1961, the enactment of the Delaware River Basin Compact enabled a dramatic change in the efforts of the Delaware River Conservation. This law brought the combined efforts of the federal government and neighboring states together as a team for the "planning, development and regulatory oversight to try and save a river using the concept of regional rather than individual municipality management."

The Delaware River Basin Compact enabled a unified approach to river conservation whereas prior to their formation, over seventy separate factional groups worked individually in their separate ways to manage the river. The DRBC, which eliminated political boundaries so to speak, is comprised of groups from New York, New Jersey, Pennsylvania and the U.S. Department of the Interior.

According to the UD Council, "in 1967, the DBRC adopted the most comprehensive water quality standards of any interstate river basin in the nation." In 1968, the DBRC created regulations to enforce these strict guidelines. The cleanup of the Delaware River basin is considered by many to be the premier success story of river management and pollution control. The unified approach of the various governmental agencies to achieve a common goal should be used as a model approach in the water management throughout the country if not the world.

Water releases to maintain an ideal trout habitat on the Delaware River is a constant source of concern. I mentioned before that NYS DEC has an agreement with NYC for conservation releases to maintain flows, especially during the hot summer months, to establish trout habitat. Each year, a certain amount of water in the reservoir is earmarked for this purpose because although the 1954 Supreme Court Decree stipulates that water releases are to be made and established at Montague and Trenton. In which case, NYS DEC can call for water releases that were earmarked for this specific purpose.

Many feel that there is a need for conservation releases during the winter months as well. Anchor ice is a proven killer of trout and minimum water levels must be established in order to ward off any ice build-up.

Two new valves were installed in the fall of 1996 that enabled a more precise adjustment of water releases from the Cannonsville Reservoir. In the old days, a release of 325 cfs was made in order to meet the requirement of 200 cfs. Now,

The NYS DEC feels that rainbow trout in the Delaware warrant special consideration because of their genetic uniqueness. It would be difficult to maintain a sizeable population of large rainbows without implementing a catch-and-release program in special trophy sections.

The Delaware valley is home to many species of wildlife. Sound conservation measures have helped to maintain water-quality standards and sustain wildlife populations.

Trout in the Delaware are wild. Many anglers resist the need for stocking, which would hamper the wild-trout populations.

releases are made as small as 45 cfs up to 325 cfs, thus allowing more water to be conserved and not wasted through inefficient flows.

In *Hatches II*, Caucci and Nastassi claim that, "anglers should object and resist stocking programs by state and federal agencies on rich rivers that support wild trout. Stockings will generally deteriorate the native population, causing the large wild fish to move out of the area rather than compete with dumb, pellet-fed hatchery fish. Hatchery survivors also have a deleterious effect on the wild strains of fish during reproduction. By the same token, fly-fishermen can't expect a wild-fish population to hold its own if it is heavily fished by meat fishermen, so true sporting anglers should push for a reduced limit of catch-and-release waters. On rivers like the Delaware system, we believe that the 12 or 13 inch to 20 inch fish should be completely protected."

The NYS DEC seems to support this contention when they write in the 1992 report, "A Fishery Management Plan for the Upper Delaware Tailwaters," that rainbow trout in the Delaware River deserve special "consideration" because of their genetic uniqueness. They say, "unlike many rainbow trout strains that exhibit migratory tendencies, self-sustaining populations of the Delaware rainbows produce trophy-size fish that remain available to anglers throughout the open season on trout. Large rainbows are also highly esteemed by

anglers because of their great strength and spectacular leaping ability. The popularity of rainbow trout is enhanced by their high catchability." The DEC maintains that because they are easy to catch, it would be very difficult to support a population of larger fish unless regulations are enforced to protect them. Catch and release should be practiced on all rainbow trout that are managed in the "trophy" trout areas.

The future of the Delaware River and its fishery is filled with optimism. However, there are certain factors that are of concern. Firstly, drought conditions could bring severe restrictions on water releases. Without sufficient water flows from the reservoirs, river temperatures will become unsuitable for trout habitation. That is, in the summer months, the river system is fully dependent on cold-water flows from the bottom-releasing reservoirs. Without it, trout simply cannot survive.

Another concern that is of paramount importance is development (and therefore potential pollution) along the river. Human encroachment puts pressures on the river's ecosystem and raises certain environmental concerns. Since the upper Delaware is only two hours from New York City, the river is a popular site for summer homes.

We must learn from our mistakes of the past and do what it takes to preserve and protect what Ernest Schwiebert calls the best in the East.

Drought conditions could bring severe restrictions on water releases. Without sufficient water flows from the reservoirs, river temperatures will become unsuitable for trout like this brown trout taken from the main stem.

Books

1. Caucci, Al & Bob Nastassi, *Hatches II*, 1986
2. Francis, Austin M, *Catskill Rivers: Birthplac*
3. Ross, John, *Trout Unlimited's Guide To Ame...* ...ing
4. Schwiebert, Ernest, *Trout*, 1978, EP Dutton
5. Swisher, Doug, *Selective Trout*, 1971, Crown Publishers

Periodicals

1. Upper Delaware Council, *The Upper Delaware*, P.O. Box 192, Narrowsburg, NY 12764, (845) 252-3022
2. The Eagle Institute, *Eagle Watch*, P.O. Box 182, Barryville, NY 12719

Studies

1. "A History Of The Fishery Resources In The Upper Delaware Tailwaters From 1800-1983," Region 4 fisheries office NYS of environmental conservation, Stanford, NY 12167, March, 1990
2. "A Fishery Management Plan For The Upper Delaware Tailwaters," Region 4 NYS Dec, March 1992
3. "A Draft Fishery Management Plan For The Upper Delaware Tailwaters. Summery of Public Response," Region 4 NYS Dec.
4. "Delaware Radiotelemetry Study, Trout Movements In The Beaverkill-Delaware Watershed," David A. Langan, PHD.

Area Fly Shops and Guiding Services

Al's Wild Trout Ltd.
HC 89 Box 666
Shinhopple, NY 13755
(607)363-7135
www.catskill.net/alstrout.com

Joe McFadden's Fly &
Tackle Shop
Rt. 97
Hankins, NY 12726
(845)887-6000
www.mcfaddensflyandtackle.com

River Essentials
HC1
Box 1025
Starlight, PA 18461
(570)635-5900
www.riveressentials.com

Area Fly Shops with Lodging and Guiding Services

Al Caucci's Delaware
River Club
HC 1 Box 1290
Starlight, PA 18461
(800)6MAYFLY
www.mayfly.com

Delaware River Fly Shop, Inc.
Rt. 191
Starlight, PA 18461
(570)635-5983

West Branch Angler &
Sportsman Resort
150 Faulkner Rd.
Deposit, NY 13754
(607)467-5525
www.westbranchangler.com

Guides

Anthony
Gone Fis
20 Lake
Narrows
(845)252

Bill Frazi
Upper Delaware Outfitters
Box 1
Hankins, NY 12741
(845)887-4853

Jerry Hadden's Guide Service
33 East River St.
Susquehanna, PA
(570)853-4048

Jim Serio
Grey Ghost Guides & Flies
118 Main St.
Hancock, NY 13783
(607)637-3474

Motels

Beaver-Dell Hotel, Inc.
Old Route 17
East Branch, NY
(607)363-7443

Capra Inn Motel
103 W. Main St.
Hancock, NY 13783
(607)637-1600

Green Acres Motel
...

Route 97
Hancock, NY 13783
(607)467-2042

Campgrounds

Catskill Mountain
Kampground
Route 30
Downsville, NY
(607)363-2599

Deer Run Rustic Campground
Route 97
Narrowsburg, NY
(845)252-7419

Delaware Valley Campsite
Route 30
Downsville, NY
(607)363-2306

Lander's River Trips
State Route 97
Narrowsburg, NY
(845) 252-3925

Peaceful Valley Campsite
Banker Road
Downsville, NY
(607)363-2211

Red Barn Campgrounds
Route 97
Hankins, NY
(845)887-4995

Soaring Eagle Campground
RR 1
Equinunk, PA
(570)224-4666

Terry's Shinhopple
Campgrounds
Route 30
East Branch, NY
(607)363-2536

Upper Delaware
Campgrounds
Creamery Road
Callicoon, NY
(845)887-5110

Thorax Sulphur

**No-Hackle
Sulphur**

**No-Hackle
Paraleptophlebia**

**No-Hackle
Blue-Winged Olive**

**Thorax
Light Cahill**

**Comparadun
Small Sulphur**

**Comparadun
Small Sulphur**

**Thorax
Heptagenia**

**Comparadun
Light Cahill**

**Extended Body
Blue-Winged Olive**

**Comparadun
Blue-Winged Olive**

**Comparadun
Blue-Winged Olive**

**CDC Comparadun
Sulphur**

**RS2
Blue-Winged Olive**

**CDC Comparadun
Sulphur**

CDC Comparadun

**Comparadun
Paraleptophlebia**

**Thorax
Paraleptophlebia**

**Thorax
Paraleptophlebia**

**Comparadun
Extended Body Sulphur**

**Comparadun
Sulphur**

**Comparadun Large
Blue-Winged Olive**

**Thorax
March Brown**

**Comparadun
Green Drake**

**Comparadun
Quill Gordon**